BE THE DJ OF YOUR CAREER

BE THE DJ OF YOUR CAREER

RODNEY JENKINS

NEW DEGREE PRESS

COPYRIGHT © 2020 RODNEY JENKINS

All rights reserved.

BE THE DJ OF YOUR CAREER

ISBN

978-1-63676-622-5   *Paperback*

978-1-63676-301-9   *Kindle Ebook*

978-1-63676-302-6   *Digital Ebook*

CONTENTS

ACKNOWLEDGEMENTS

When setting out on a long journey you've never embarked on before, you never know how much work it will take to reach your final destination. I've discovered along my journey writing *Be the DJ of Your Career* that publishing a book takes a village, and I am so grateful for all of the support. Fulfilling this dream would not have been possible without you.

Thank you first and foremost to my Mom and Dad for your supporting me through every step of the way, always.

And thank you to everyone who: gave me their time for a personal interview, pre-ordered the eBook, paperback, and multiple copies to make publishing possible, helped spread the word about *Be the DJ of Your Career* to gather amazing momentum, and helped me publish a book I am proud of. I am sincerely grateful for all of your help.

Denise Knowles	Sharon Gibson
Willie Speaks III	Zauresh Kezheneva
Paul Swanson	Helen Tomosoiu

Ida Habtemichael

Helen Bidol

Xiaofang Li

Lillian Moultrie

Kyle Szklenski

Charlotte Hine

Madeline Stueber

Julie Bostian

Martha Huang

Hillary Garber

Siddharth Singh

Zonta Owens

Kasey Stricklin

Angela Long

Enyioma Obiakara

DJ Flocka

Mihyun Yun

Tanisha Jenkins

Kendrick Jenkins

Sharon Gibson

Paula Finkelstein

Mary Kitson

Sabrina Icahn

Zhaochun Tan

Venkat Viswanathan

Linda Hoyt

Venencia Magnusen

Jasmine Yeung

Kelly Rohrer

Kevin MacWhorter

Scott Nahrgang

Adriana Gomes

Flavio Gavao

Mark Carr

Beatrice Jenkins

Maceo Jenkins

Drew Tschetter

Alexia Stewart

DJ Kim

Tyrone Jenkins

PREFACE

Be the DJ of Your Career is a book that walks the reader through a series of interview-style conversations with random people about what they are doing to manage their careers. The reference to DJs is due to my fascination and belief they—for the most part—seem to live, breathe, sleep, and re-awaken with relentless ingenuity, grit, and resourcefulness in a way that grows and compounds success in their career. This book touches upon that during the myriad of random conversations.

Long before starting a job, quitting a job, getting fired (or laid off), or taking a very extended vacation (vis-à-vis, medical leave), you may venture out to talk with some trusted friends or a few deeply loving family members; or better yet, maybe you sought the advice of a career coach. Yeah, well, I have been there, too. Over the years, I have personally experienced or heard, some of the following career challenges to one's career:

- I don't want to beat around the bush, but I think my boss is sabotaging my chances of being promoted. She is constantly barking at me. How should I deal with this?

- I complained about my unfair workload, and suddenly received a written warning for my poor performance on a project. I have been doing the job of two people and have been putting in lots of hours on my weekends. What the hell should I do about this?

- What I am actually doing in this job is different from what was explained in the job interview and on the position description. What should I do?

- I can't stand working anymore with my co-workers. One of them is constantly underperforming or is simply late each time on his portion of the project, and we need to step in to complete it. What should I do about this?

- My position was downsized, and I am out of work. I have been applying everywhere for two months, yet I haven't received any responses. My emergency savings and fistful of credit cards will be on the other side of "zero" in three months. What are your thoughts on what I can do to land a good job?

- I just started this job, but I don't want to work here anymore. I will stick it out for a few months until I can find something else.

- For the last eight months, I was told that I am doing well, and now as we near the annual performance review, I am told that I am not doing that well. I am so confused! I need to get another job before I am fired or laid off. Fuck them!

Real talk! The work it takes to get, keep, and leave a career position, job, or gig is incredibly hard. For some, the challenges seem to press play, repeat, press play, repeat, and press play, repeat throughout our career lives. And for others, we work, stress, and deal with the shark-infested waters of the workplace until we retire or change jobs.

[Insert your scream-laced profanity here] I share your anguish, pain, and the sense of mind-numbing perplexity. No amount of Starbucks coffee or tea or wine will ease the pain, but I certainly encourage you to try. Also, while you are sufficiently trying that, please get in a comfortable chair and read my short book. I hope that it serves to inspire you and lighten your perspective and may the list of resources prove helpful to you and anyone you know.

The late great *Black Panther* actor Chadwick Boseman said in a Commencement Speech at Howard University, "Purpose crosses disciplines. Purpose is an essential element of you. It is the reason that you are on this planet at this particular time in history."[1] I deeply believe we need to orient ourselves on what drives our happiness, peace, and sense of achievement in our homes, in our work lives, and in our relationships with others. I don't want to live to work. I want to work to help me live the life I am determined to have. I think everyone needs to define what is "purpose" and "meaning" in their lives, and how to manage a career that aligns with your purpose as much as possible.

---

1   Chadwick Boseman, "Commencement Speech: What You Fight For," May 12, 2018.

CHAPTER 1

BALINDA

Balinda: What's up, Rodney?

Rodney: I am ok. How are you, Balinda?

Balinda: Just struggling with this job search...it is kicking my ass. Leaving Jersey was the best thing that I have ever done, but I never thought that I would have so much trouble finding a decent job in Washington, DC. I have applied to over one hundred positions online in two months.

Rodney: Yeah, I hear you. Just started my contract job, but now I am told that the six-month contract will be shortened to three months.

Balinda: Who did you piss off? She asks before leaving my table to get coffee. We arrived early, but the line inside Panera Bread is starting to form.

Balinda and I moved to the Washington, DC about the same time. She is the first in her family to have completed college. Balinda is a Latina in her early thirties with a passion for graphic design and a fiery determination to succeed. She claims her cooking is as good as her graphic designing skills. Maybe she should look for a cooking job, but I don't suggest it... I know it would piss her off.

We met in the line at this Panera Bread about four months ago. The day we met she was dressed in a smart suit with hip dark red shoes. She is a good friend and we have learned from each other in this frustrating journey to land a job. She graduated with honors in Digital Communication from a university in New Jersey and worked as a communications consultant for two companies. Balinda's one-page resume was professionally reviewed by a resume expert, yet despite spending $200 to get it professionally "blinged" up, she hasn't landed any jobs. Scoring interviews isn't her problem, but actually to get an offer is the problem. I couldn't understand it. Practice, practice, and more interview practice is what we did for each interview she landed, yet no job.

Fast Forward... two months later...

I receive a call from Balinda during my fifteen-minute lunch break.

Balinda: Rodney, I got great news!

Rodney: Cool. What is it?

Balinda: I received a job offer from a consulting firm.

Over the next few minutes, Balinda shares the details about a contract-to-hire position that pays about half of the salary that she earned in Jersey. Honestly, I am happy that she landed a job, but what the hell for half the salary that she earned in Newark.

Rodney: Did you accept?

Balinda: Of course, Mr. Potato Head. *I guess my head is shaped like a potato.*

Rodney: Ok, cool.

Over the next four months, Balinda worked harder than the energizer bunny to blaze a path to a permanent job. I mean, she was working over fifty-five hours per week. I was confident she was going to be offered a permanent position, but instead, her contract was extended for another three months, and then extended again. After ten months at the firm, she was let go. She had put her life on hold to focus entirely on this low-paying job, and now she was forced to begin the job search process over again with no connections, no severance, and no clue on how to find and keep a job in one of the most competitive cities in the world. What a freaking nightmare!

The job market has always been competitive, but it is seems so many qualified people, like Balinda, are not only finding it difficult to land a good-paying job, but also keeping one— especially a job that pays full benefits. According to Glassdoor's research, on average, every private sector job opening attracts 250 resumes, but only four to six of these people will be called for an interview, and only one of those will be offered a job. Furthermore, according to Glassdoor, 80% of job seekers use social media to conduct their job search.[2] Balinda's situation is common based on Glassdoor's data, so

---

2   "50 HR and Recruiting Stats that Make You Think," Glassdoor, published January 20, 2015.

in order to increase her odds dramatically she must deploy a multi-pronged approach to land a job faster. If I were to break down the statistics—which I will do in the next chapter—by demographics between women and men, and minority groups, you will begin to see a pattern emerge in the overall spectrum of this struggle to find and keep a job.

Back to Balinda, she eventually gave up with the search for a job in Washington, DC, and the surrounding cities, and moved back to Newark to live with two friends in a small apartment. It took her another six months, but she was hired as a marketing specialist for a large engineering firm. Luckily, she got help from a former professor she had reached out to.

It is sad Balinda, like so many people with a dream of living a comfortable life in the big city, are in for a rude awakening when they discover how incredibly exhausting, frustrating, and soul draining it can be to pursue, maintain, and thrive according to your American dream. It is easy enough to find roommates and live in a shared house until you can spread your wings to live on your own. Now, the ugly reality is to live the "nice" life—with a nice condo or townhouse (ain't going broke trying to purchase a single family home), nice job, and nice friends—it is nice to think about achieving, but it is very difficult to get and sustain at that level.

So many of us need help on how to not only reach the career dream or high paying job, but how to manage our work lives in a way that aligns with our vision of success, happiness, purpose, and peace in our work lives or hustle.

CHAPTER 2

DIGGING INTO SOME STATISTICS, SOME COACHING, AND SOME PIZZA

The problem of feeling unhappy, disengaged, and generally frustrated with one's job is a staggering issue that affects every sector of the global economy. The Conference Board reports that 53% of Americans are currently unhappy at work.[3] Let's ponder that for a moment. For every person that has a job in the US about half are not happy in their job. In a Deloitte report, they indicated that 80% of people do not like their jobs. Since a lot of us spend at least 40 hours a week of their lives at work, this is a significant problem. Another global consulting and research firm called Gallup indicated in the 2013 research report that only 11% of all employees are "highly

---

3   The Conference Board, "Job Satisfaction: 2014 Edition," The Conference Board Job Satisfaction Survey, 2014.

engaged" and 24% are "actively disengaged."[4] With the reality of this issue hitting the revenue of so many companies in every country, a concrete solution has been evasive, but the response of the professional coaching industry has proved helpful in addressing the need of workers who are trying to improve their lives at work, or for those who seek advice and guidance as they change jobs.

According to the International Federation of Coaching (IFC), they predict that the total market forecast for coaching is expected to grow by annual rate of 5.4%until 2022.[5] Equally interesting, the IFC's global membership has grown more than 100% since 2010 in reaction to the global demand for coaching. While this statistic reflects the surge in demand for career coaching, it also underscores the challenge employers face in finding a way to sufficiently reduce employee disengagement, unhappiness, and frustration. Over my years as a volunteer career coach, I have been shocked by the extent some workers have tried to resolve their work issues—whether performance, communication conflicts, and not feeling part of the "work family." In my own career, I have noticed my ability to feel successful, engaged, and happy was directly correlated to the degree I had a good relationship with my manager and co-workers. Spending so much time in the office (or virtually...well, unfortunately, this is October 2020, and so the COVID-19 pandemic has forced so many to work remotely)._

---

4   Steve Crabtree, "Worldwide, 13% of Employees Are Engaged at Work," State of the Global Workplace, 2019.

5   Your Coach, "Health Coaching Industry Report," Health Coach Industry Report: Aiding at the Frontlines of Health (2019): 14.

In Daniel Pink's national bestseller, *Drive*, he writes people are driven by, "autonomy, mastery, and purpose."[6] He argues that supporting employees will require the following three areas in order to achieve a higher level of performance and on-the-job satisfaction: autonomy, mastery, and purpose. A breakdown of each area includes the following:

- Autonomy—our desire to be self-directed which results in increased engagement over compliance. [Think: DJ is the self-directed and free to move in a way that keeps them engaged]

- Mastery—the urge to get better skills. [Think: DJs are constantly working to refine and improve their skills]

- Purpose The desire to do something that has meaning and is important. It is not a focus on the revenue, but it is about valuing your employee, customers, and vendors, and also creating a sense of mission. [Think: DJs are incredibly focused on creating a fantastic experience for everyone in the room. Well, yeah, they will get $$. They want you to be deeply and emotionally moved.]

I share Daniel Pink's perspective. I have felt the pain points in a career job when I felt there was little autonomy, and/or not enough mastery of the skills, and/or no sense of purpose (i.e. not feeling any sort of mission). On the other hand, I have experienced the benefits of working in jobs where all three areas where positively present. Actually, I remember

---

6   Daniel H. Pink, *Drive: The Surprising Truth About What Motivates Us* (New York: Riverhead Books, 2009).

when I worked at Pizza Hut as a pizza maker, and absolutely loved working there on a part-time basis for two years. The manager Blaine and his wife Jennifer, head waitress, managed the super busy restaurant. I was trained, tested on the slower shifts, and asked to pretend I was training the head manager on how to perform my job.

Once someone had been thoroughly trained, tested, and "pretended" to train the manager on their job as a pizza maker effectively, the trainee would be moved to the fast-paced shift. As a pizza maker, I worked hard to make the best pizza while laughing at jokes, growing closer to my co-workers with each life story we shared while working, and enjoying the mandatory two fifteen-minute breaks and a thirty-minute lunch break. For a great shift's work, the manager would award a free pizza to the team member who performed the best in the kitchen. Because I proved myself, I was given so much autonomy in the kitchen, and felt the confidence the managers and other staff had in me when we worked together. Lastly, I felt such a deep degree of purpose because we had staff meetings where we discussed our role in achieving the business' goal, and celebrated our victories with pictures, success stories, and bi-monthly dinner parties at the head manager's house or another co-worker's house.

On my last day on the job, I was watery-eyed, and looked to the team where silence fell across the room during the final minutes of the farewell party. Before I left for the night, I was given a large box. I opened it and found a red Pizza Hut jacket with everyone's name handwritten on the inside. Now, I have had many jobs since that one, but I believe my Pizza Hut experience is the best one to reflect on the beauty of when all three areas are positively manifested in the work we do.

CHAPTER 3

WHY ARE DJS SO INTERESTING?

———

Let's reword the question a bit: why are DJs so interesting to most people? For a lot of music fans, they are the creative entertainment mega-machine everyone listens to, responds to, and is most engaged by at a birthday party, night club, wedding, or neighborhood rooftop party. If you think about it, a DJ was the music-producing puppet master along with its social mixologist sidekick, alcohol, that chilled the nerves so that your parents could strike up a conversation, and then turning the initial socialization into something more romantic. As I sit here writing, my head glistens with chill vibes because I am listening to a mix of music on YouTube by Jabig, who is a popular Canadian DJ. He is currently on a historic first DJ world tour by bicycle in a five-year epic journey to fulfill a life-long dream to raise money for World Bicycle Relief—a charity that has distributed close to 500,000 bikes in Western Africa.

JaBig is a talented and inspiring DJ artist, to the say the least. So, DJs are doing some amazing things in their essence with music, but also in other ways to help people outside of music. Isn't that cool? What is even more interesting is DJs are actually artists that build their business, build their presence, style, and brand, while managing all aspects of achieving success in an extremely competitive and ever-changing market. They need to build and maintain a deep knowledge of how to leverage their knowledge, skills, and abilities in a way to maximize their market presence. In the case of JaBig, he is constantly building his brand through YouTube. The world tour charity serves to benefit others but allows him to further build a wider audience/market.

The universe of the DJ is an ecosystem filled with their ever-flowing network of partners, musical artists, good friends, DJs, and other business associates. But, as we dig a bit deeper, I see this world is exhaustingly competitive, lightning fast-paced, and dynamically changes to keep pace with the demands of the customer, audience, and unexpected surprises. They have developed a real-time entrepreneur mindset, which keeps them growth-minded so they can achieve their goals.

Yes, they are often popular. Well, they need to be popular, flexible, versatile, and well liked on many different levels. In other words, their career success depends on their ability to build relationships with people and stay in constant alignment with their customers, i.e. the crowd. If they are dynamic in all the right ways, new DJing opportunities can be shared through their customers. It is a fine art to a DJ's method of building their brand, and therefore, building the successful outcomes for which they aspire. Because of their approach, grit, and growth-centered mindset, I think there are many things anyone in a career can learn from the DJ industry.

As a volunteer career coach for many years, I feel there is a great need for more inspiring and creative stories to awaken the "working" reader to the reality that they have more power than they realize to transform, energize, and move their career forward or move it into a new direction. After you read this book, my hope is you will realize you control the music, you have the ability to influence others (DJ would say "move the crowd"), and you have the power to move your career in new directions. It is the creative, resourceful, gritty, "out of box" thinker, aka "the inner DJ," that needs to take residence in your mind and soul to help you reach deeper into yourself to guide you on taking the right steps to manage your career. I want you to see this book as an opportunity to be a fly on the wall so you can witness purpose-driven conversations about how others manage their careers, escape the mundane of what you know, and let us learn something from a few DJs and other engaging personalities so we will be able to gain a deeper sense of inspiration and career insight, too.

CHAPTER 4

CONVERSATION WITH DJ FLOCKA

After connecting with DJ Flocka on Linkedin, I tried to call him a few times and emailed the questions. He was quick with getting back to me. I have reached out to nearly forty DJs and interviewed a few but felt DJ Flocka's interview was interesting and descriptive. He was cool and generous on sharing his thoughts about his rise as a DJ.

DJ Flocka: It is good that we can connect over the phone. The questions that you emailed were weird. It is always better to talk with people.

Rodney: I agree. Those questions are generally specific so I can capture as much information as possible. I am new at the interview thing. What do you as a DJ?

DJ Flocka: I play a mix of music for crowds in nightclubs, private parties, lounges, or at any event for a client. I play off the energy of the crowd and hit them with music that I know that they want to hear. I've been in this game for a long time. I got in to DJing about ten years ago. I have been able to branch out into other things, such as music production, hosting a radio show, public spots, and private parties

Rodney: How do you grow your DJ skills?

DJ Flocka: It ain't just about playing and spinning mixed music. I need to be a creative machine first and foremost. Anyone can organize a party and set themselves up as the DJ at that party. But, if you are serious in this competitive business, you need to think about how to try new songs, and new ways to mix and play the music. The crowd is your teacher, they tell you what is good, and let you know what they don't like.

Rodney: How do you know if the crowd is feeling what you are playing?

DJ Flocka: The crowds yells out, dance, people stay, and nod their heads.

Rodney: How did you know that you wanted to be a DJ?

DJ Flocka: I started as a DJ about ten years... I rented some DJ equipment, got a scratchboard, and then worked my way up to more equipment. I kept pushing the creativity to do more.

Rodney: How do grow your business? How do you know who can help you to grow?

DJ Flocka: Well, it is always about partnering. I mean, it is about finding and getting people to support what you are doing, and they get a cut. Also, when I find young artists, I play their music, and expand into more partnerships. Some early gigs were $50, and nowadays I get some for $10K to $50K. Once people get to know you, they talk, and they call you about gigs.

Rodney: How do you learn?

DJ Flocka: I learn by trying new music out and being as creative as I can. I constantly push to take the music to the next level and use my creativity and understanding of what people like to get me there. If it is good, the audience will definitely let me know. This profession is like building a house, you create a strong foundation of your skills through quality equipment, expand on social media every day (I am talking Instagram, Facebook, and YouTube), and if you're doing good in a gig, they will ask you to come back, and then referrals, and the business partners will always give you more leads.

Rodney: How do you hustle in the work that you do?

DJ Flocka: Outside of the DJing, I host a show on a radio station in Jacksonville and get a ton of new artists that reach out to me to play their music, and then I connect with off-air, too.

The DJ industry is not hard to get in to, but it is very competitive, as you expand into higher paying gigs. It is like getting on a basketball team—you work hard to get on the team, but then you need to work your ass off to stay on the team, and so you need to prove yourself every time you play. The best players stay on the team and may move into the NBA, where the payout, and potentially business relationships are bigger. It is hard to stay in this profession and not get knocked out of your perch because you can't just book the right mix of good paying clients and partners that can help you win more of the higher paying business. You are building a reputation, and a DJ's reputation is everything. You have to use creativity to always elevate your game even when you think no one is listening.

CHAPTER 5

MEDITATION CLASS

———

For the last few years, I have been using meditation apps—Calm and Headspace—to get me into the meditation groove. I feel so much clarity, ease of focus, and water-like flow of energy for a few hours after it is done. About a year, I found an interesting meditation center in Tyson's Corner called Medita tion Museum. They have a great parking lot and intimidating stairs to climb to the upper level where it is located—but it is well worth the climb. You enter an oasis of tranquil music, warm smiles, and an intricately decorated lobby that has plush carpeting and radiates a smell of lavender. Meditation Muscum is bubbling with positive energy that strangely feels like I can breathe easier because I think the oxygen level is somehow higher in their center. I try to go there at least 3 times a month, and then rely on the meditation apps about four times a week.

Well, tonight's class was amazing. I tried to clear my mind for class, but my mind keeps moving back to focusing on what does it take to "Be the DJ of Your Career." This statement, or rather the question—what does it take to be the DJ of Your Career—is definitely a truly exciting concept that casts a spell on my normally meditative mind, and has entered my sacred meditation space, too. As I prepare to leave tonight's class, I strike up a conversation with one of the other newer students.

Rodney: What a great class tonight. I think you are new to our class? I am Rodney.

Vishnu: I am, Vishnu. Yes, I am. I used to meditate all the time back home. He puts on a NY Yankees baseball cap.

Rodney: NYC?

Vishnu: No, I am from Montreal, Canada.

Rodney: Cool. Where did you study meditation in Montreal?

Vishnu: Centre de Meditation Kadampa in Montreal. I studied there for many years. It is a beautiful and tranquil place. The teachers were kind, deeply understanding, and helpful.

Rodney: How did you hear about the Meditation Museum here in Tyson's Corner?

Vishnu: A co-worker told me about it.

Rodney: We leave the building and continue talking in the parking lot. How does meditation help you at work? What do you do exactly?

Vishnu: I am a mechanical engineer for a large government contractor in Bethesda. Yeah, it is one of those fast-paced, high demand, and no time for a lunch break sort of places to work. Since I have been practicing meditation for a long time, I find it helps me to relax and control my emotional steering wheel. My car is the body, and the road ahead is what I deal with every day at work. I drove for a private limousine company in Toronto while in college, and realized I can't control people or what I need to deal with on my drive to pick them up, but I can decide and train my mind, body, and spirit on how I choose to react to the crazy shit that comes my way.

Rodney: That's deep. So, the mind controls the emotions, and everything inside you? Do you have bad days and things that stress you out?

Vishnu: Not so much at work. I have been with this employer a little over a year. I expect co-workers will call out on a dead-line intensive project and know the boss will constantly push more work, and more work on us all the time. But I have made it a practice to build positive energy, which mainly involves sharing funny stories, references to interesting scenes in movies, collaborating on problem-solving walks to stimulate clear thinking, and never eating alone whenever I take a lunch break. Actually, I enjoy the craziness at work, and just keep shifting the emotional steering wheel. It is cool.

Rodney: It has been great talking with you. I am writing a book about being the DJ of your career, which refers to a belief that we have the power to build and manage a successful career while navigating the gritty rollercoaster ride of the ups and downs in the job market along the way. So, I am wondering if you believe that you are DJ of your career? If so, why, how, and what keeps you in that mindset?

Vishnu: Oh, man. It is so cool you are writing this book. I am intrigued. Will our conversation be included in the book?

Rodney: Yes. You ok with that?

Vishnu: Ok, that is fine. Well, I do believe I am the DJ of my career, at least my wife thinks so. Just kidding. *We laugh.* My father was a farmer in India, and he worked harder than anyone that I have ever known. My two brothers and I helped with some of the farming when we didn't have homework or chores to finish in the house. He easily worked seventy to eighty hours a week. Despite his exhaustion, he took time to learn about our daily life, how we endured very long walks to school, even in the monsoons. His eyes were like fire, as he seemed to be so consumed with a burning interest to understand and respond with wonderfully positive advice. Looking back, I know some days, he was fighting exhaustion, but still would talk until very late. So, the foundation of everything of who I am was born out of those experiences with loving and incredibly hard-working parents, who served as role models. My parents were the DJs of their careers, and the whole community knew it. So, I grew up in such a shadow of them to become who I am today. I enjoy the pain of days that I work until midnight, pain of difficult projects, and difficult co-workers on occasion, but I know it is for a greater glory that allows me to provide a nice home for my family, a future for my kids, and the occasional yoga or meditation class. Rodney, I enjoyed our conversation, brotha. I got to head home before the wife sends a search party to look for me. Looking forward to seeing you in this class next week. We shake hands and I slowly walk to my car.

Sitting in my car, my head is filled with the vibes from a great class and conversation. While I found I was so aligned with focus and raindrop-like clarity with each deep breath, I found I was equally moved by the conversation with Vishnu. Being emotionally self-aware and fully appreciative of his parent's work ethic seem to have nurtured a keen sense of purpose and self-sacrifice for the substance of life, which is most important to him. I think the emotional stirring wheel is a power analogy to think about the reality that there is so much in life that pull, push, and trigger emotional shifts at any given time. So, hell yes, the need to develop focus and awareness to better respond is vital to everyone seeking to be the DJ of their career. I think our meditation teacher would agree with Vishnu's emotional stirring wheel perspective, though she would certainly present a meditative approach that involves emptying the mind and improving focus in order to see clearly what should be done in situations that challenge our emotional control and reaction.

CHAPTER 6

CONVERSATIONS WITH RANDOM PEOPLE IN JAKE'S COFFEE SHOP

———

Getting away for the three-day Labor Day weekend is exactly what I needed. Work can be so exhausting, and my workload has been crippling, to say the least. Luckily, I was able to book a roundtrip ticket on the Mega-bus to NYC. I grabbed a seat on the upper deck towards the front of the crowded and lively bus. Hearing the chatter of college students, families, and professionals escaping the concrete jungle of DC fills the air with excitement and relaxation. My mind doesn't want to let go from figuring out how to talk with more people and build my pages of the book with more great content. I feel like *Be the DJ of Your Career*, is my odyssey. Yep, so far, it has been a true journey of insightful, sometimes painful conversations, self-discoveries, adventures, and various challenges along my way to its end. Yeah, I realize I am not necessarily searching for something or a way to get back home like Odysseus, yet I can't help but feel I am on a journey, which ultimately lands me in a different place once I reach the end.

Am I nervous? Am I doubtful? Am I uncertain whether I can complete this book? Yes, I am, but I believe God will guide, empower, and enlighten me on every step of this crazy, exhausting, and soulful journey. I strive to maintain focus, courageousness, and a sense of gratitude for the generosity of others to reflect, share, and provide their perspectives I never would have imagined or learned on my own. I doze off for a few hours, then wake up suddenly to the bus driver announcing we are about 30 minutes away from the Manhattan bus terminal. I put on my headphones and let the smooth, mixed rhythms of DJ Khaled blast into my ears. My head is nodding, and I can feel the sparking feeling of excitement and wonder as we draw closer to the terminal. "New York City, I am ready to make this a great weekend, enjoy some great DJ mixes, slam a few slices of pizzas down my throat, and spark up some random conversations with people for my book (I am talking to myself in a low voice, because I'm crazy like that as I look out the window into the magic lights of Manhattan)."

Hotel Moxy is my favorite all-in-one spot for sleep, dining, and the roof-top music scene is dope! Waking up early is what I do best, and so I swing the hotel's entrance door hard as I walk out on to the sidewalk. I walk through Times Square to Jake's Coffee Shop in the Knickerbocker Hotel. That is my spot for great tea and a crusty blueberry muffin. While my tea is being prepared, I take a seat at the front of the café near the main door, but not too close to feel a breeze when it opens. This place is amazing. The venue's namesake honors John Jacob "Jakey" Astor VI, son of hotel founder John Jacob Astor IV, born just four months after his father died on the Titanic. The Café has a vaulted barrel ceiling and stylish interiors fashioned in textural overtones. Because of this history, vaulted ceilings, and just a few blocks away from Times Square, this is a popular and relaxing café that screams, "come inside, chill and get to know one another in our fine establishment."

I place a standing placard on my table, which is facing the main entrance, it reads, "Be the DJ of Your Career" in large, bold letters, and in smaller letters, it reads "Free Your Conversation – Managing Your Career Well?" Because there is essentially a long runway before you get to the counter/cashier, it would be difficult for Café's staff to spot my placard, and unless I annoy a customer, I should be ok to talk to a lot of people at my makeshift public office in a very public coffee shop for a good while.

My name is called. I walk down the runway to pick up my large cup of tea and blueberry muffin. I am feeling all kinds of positive energy, creativity, and excitement. Energy is the least of what I need as I smile and look up to someone standing in front of my placard.

CHAPTER 7

JESSIE

Rodney: Good morning. I introduce myself and smile too big. My over eager smile made her flinch a bit, but she is so damn cool that she responds with a half smirk and carefully keeps her coffee cup in a sort of protective posture to keep me and my big smile at a forced distance away.

Jessie: Nice placard. So, what is this all about?

Rodney: I am working on my first book, and I am starting to realize that I feel asleep when I try to get into research for my topic, and also it will take too long to gather great content from interviewing people the traditional way—which means finding people who are available, and also scheduling a time [which invariably they need to reschedule anyway... let's be real about how difficult it is to schedule interviews] that fits their availability. So, I came up with a radical idea to put myself out there by just going to a few public places to mix with people in the "wild." Thank you for stopping here. These conversations are unscripted, but I have some questions to ask you. Is that cool?

Jessie: Yes, hit me your questions, Mr. Career DJ.

Rodney: What do you do? And please tell me how you are the DJ of your career.

Jessie: I am the international marketing director for a large consulting firm. My boss and my team are bitchy bastards, but I don't let them wrinkle me none. I laugh a little but realize that I need to keep our voices down. I motion for Jessie to sit down, and she obliges. At twenty-nine, I was the youngest to be promoted into this position, and I turned thirty last month. I interned for a competing consulting firm while in college, and simply received a much better offer from this current firm. I was hired as a marketing specialist, and simply bust my ass, and got the freaking results that made my manager's hairy mustache wiggle on each end. My magnetic and strongly positive personality is the gift that keeps on giving. I was valued for my voice, research, and drive for turning clients into repeat customers time and time again. During my first two years, I literally worked eighty hours a week and did amazing things that slapped the consciousness of what it means to provide the best client advice to the next level.

I just keep nodding and following along with every word. I can't believe that I landed such a great interview so quickly.

Jessie: There were nine of us in the same position, and I knew that someone was going to be promoted to marketing manager. Knowing that, I reframed how I thought about my position, I start to think of it as a business development role in the marketing department. I began to initiate new business with clients, and everyone in their supply chain. I maxed out my corporate card on client dinners, personalized birthday cards, and localized business trips, including weekends. I nabbed two college interns and paid them a stipend via a personal loan. My work volume, network of connections, and business revenue was more than twice that of my fellow, always complaining colleagues. I presented a proposal to the director on a plan to triple our customer base and business revenue within twelve months. You could literally hear the "mic drop hard" when he read my proposal. This second-generation Puerto Rican in a male dominated industry was calling the shots and making many heads turn whenever I walked around in the office. So, I hope that you are taking notes, Mr. Career DJ.

Rodney: Yes, I am. I follow every word you are saying. Now, she is staring at me to encourage my focus on what she is saying, I guess. Funny thing is now I think she is playing who can blink first game. I hold my gaze for about twenty-three seconds. She smiles to let me know that she won. Damn!

Jessie: My proposal was accepted by my manager and the leadership team also agreed I would be promoted to marketing manager. I am the DJ of my career because I figured out what I wanted, delivered on my promise to self, got my interns hired as marketing specialists, and became a business leader. Funny thing is no one wanted rice and beans when I used to bring it to the office, but after I got the big promotion, they cannot get enough of it.

Rodney: Jessie, your story is amazing and inspiring. I am like "wow" and you hit them up with your rice and bean superpower. *She laughs.*

Jessie: I was promoted a second time to director after three years in the marketing manager position. My secret weapons are I go to church every Sunday, constantly built my business within the business, and am active in my Toastmaster's club.

Rodney: Toastmasters? Church? How did they help you?

Jessie: Come on, Mr. Career DJ. Alright, let me explain. Toastmasters is the largest and most committed organization to help anyone to become a great speaker, great communicator, and great interpersonal strategist. My club drops the mic every week. The club's team meeting format and the endless opportunities to practice and improve in a positive and supportive learning laboratory was more helpful than my psychology degree. Also, I became good friends with a lot of older folks who shared career advice. I think the power to listen, understand, and persuade were the weapons in my arsenal as I battled on my way to my director position. Now, church allowed me to become stronger in my faith and belief that I am blessed for a higher purpose in this firm. God was my master teacher, and oh, I learned many lessons on my journey, and I learned them best when I taught my interns how to be "mini versions of me." I started laughing again, and so did she…

Jessie: Mr. Career DJ, it was great talking with you. This was really interesting. This is my favorite coffee on this block. Here is my business card, and let's connect on Linkedin. I want a copy of the book when it is ready. Time for work. She walks down the runway and exits Jake's from back entrance (which is the Knickerbocker hotel's entrance).

CHAPTER 8

SOLOMON

———

A college student with a Columbia University pullover is curiously looking at the placard on my table. He probably studied all night because his eyes are unhealthily red and eyebags are swollen. Yep, he better sips that coffee to get a caffeine boost to stay on his feet.

Rodney: Hello? How are you? I see you are college student at Columbia.

Solomon: I'm doing ok. No, I don't attend Columbia, I just like their clothing. I work there in the evenings and on weekends. I am a part-time student at Brooklyn College. So, what is this all about?

Rodney: I am working on a book with a working title, *Be the DJ of Your Career*. So, I thought it would be a lot more interesting and engaging to strike up conversations with people who stop at this table instead of the conventional approach of finding interview candidates, and then scheduling interviews. I want to talk with people who have a proactive approach to managing their career and I want to learn how they are doing it.

Solomon: Wow, this is incredibly interesting. I want to learn how to manage my career someday. My situation is I am a struggling student, and I needed to change majors twice. Being from West Africa, I have had to overcome so much, especially learning English, and needing to figure out how to live in New York City nearly killed me. By the way, my name is Solomon. What is your name?

Rodney: I introduce myself and we shake hands. Solomon, it is good to meet you. Based on what you have shared about what you had to overcome, I know that you have what it takes to "Be the DJ of Your Career." I think that it all starts with a rock-solid sense of self-belief and a bullseye focus leveled to things that are most important to you. The famous motivational speaker, Les Brown, once said "I have learned that to get out of life what I expect, I must commit myself to beginning each day by concentrating on positive thoughts and focusing on my goals." Solomon, I think his words and how he says what he says in his speeches are so powerful in watering the seeds of anyone's ambition, self-belief, and motivation. A friend walks up to Solomon from the rear, and motions to leave.

Solomon: Rodney, thank you for taking the time to talk to me. Sorry about my friend's bitchy personality. He says it loud so she can hear, and chuckles. I will check out, Les Brown. Yeah, let's stay in touch, I want to read your book Be the DJ of Your Career! I like it! They leave slowly.

CHAPTER 9

CONNOR

I felt a cold breeze when he walked in. A typical businessman in a rush, goes to Jake's counter. I think his height contributed to the breeze effect. I can't hear what he orders, but I know it is a large coffee. Out of the corner of my eye, I see as he waits, he is slowly surveying the room, and his gaze settles on my curiously innocent table for a moment. The tall, serious man walks up the runway, and takes a seat across the aisle from my table. He unfolds a Financial Times newspaper, which seemingly was pulled directly from the inside of his pin stripe suit jacket. The coffee shop is quiet.

Honestly, I don't want this person to walk over to my table. I am thinking and hoping he finishes his coffee and folds his newspaper before leaving Jake's. I just don't think someone with such controlled movements, James Bond-like arrogance as far as I could see, and likely has a Brooks Brothers credit card, would be interesting to interview. I was wrong.

After ten minutes, the tall man finishes his paper, and enjoys his coffee. He quickly stands, brushes his lapel, and suspiciously walks over.

Connor: He speaks with a British accent and warmly smiles. He mellows out the words, Hello, my friend.

Rodney: Good morning, sir.

I smile. I tell him about why I am here, and what I seek to do with this initiative. He listens intensely. He says his name is Connor. He is a business executive with a private shipping company with offices in London, Dublin, New York, and New Orleans.

Connor: After hearing your explanation, I must say I find your book writing topic fascinating, and more accurately the strategy for building great content a great one. Your approach is engaging, and while I am generally skeptical of many things until the plan is deployed, I see potential in not only the reach of the book, but more importantly how you can inspire and help others learn how to become DJ's of their career. Cool stuff, man. What questions do you have for me?

Rodney: Are you the DJ of Your Career? How have you evolved into being the DJ of your career? Please describe your mindset around work, business, and achieving success. How do you move or influence the "crowd?" What are your techniques or devices you use to play the right music for the right impact? Let me stop there.

Connor: Do you think I have all day to answer your questions? *He waits, and then laughs.*

Rodney: Connor, I know it is a lot of open-ended questions, so feel free to provide answers to what you want to talk about. Keep in mind you will be playing a role in inspiring, educating, and shining a light on values and life lessons which have been the catalyst for the way you have moved forward in your career.

Connor: Well, well, where and how do I begin here. Let me think for a second. Growing up in The Athens of the North Edinburgh, Scotland, was anything one would call a life of easy road. Life was hard, my friend. Due to my dad's emotional depression from chronic fatigue syndrome, it seemed to have cast a shadow on my family in everything related to life. But in spite of the economic and emotional challenges of growing up, I absolutely loved Edinburgh. The vastness of the beaches, the beauty of the views from Calton Hill, and the delicious haggis alongside neeps and tatties tasted divine. The festivity and sincerity of the people in my town, Leith, were so endearing. This was the city where Sean Connery and J.K. Rowling were made. Actually, I have been to Fountainbridge where Sean grew up.

Connor: Rodney, you need to understand generally Scottish people are very tough, spirited, and believe in the power of unity. If you get the chance, please watch the movie, *Brave Heart*, which is about William Wallace, and what he fought for. Now, I must say many of the cities and towns suffer from a riddling of poverty and struggling to make the best of what we have. We are damn merry and damn good at enjoying what we have in life. If you get the chance to grab a drink with a Scot, I promise you it will be a most unforgettable experience for you. I have shared this background so you can piece together a base understanding of what forces have shaped and molded who I am as the DJ of my career. I think my drive and commitment to create a happy future for my parents and brother were the motivating forces which helped to build me.

Connor: I worked as a cleaner with my mom as far back as I can remember. My dad's chronic fatigue syndrome really screwed up his ability to hold a job. He was good with his hands, and so he could fix things around the house. Since he always drank beer heavily, his eyes seemed to shine like a doll, and his voice was shallow a lot of times. I think he found strength in drinking and fixing stuff at home. Now, I think his circumstance created a groundswell of our awakening in it for us to survive we needed to work harder and harder, especially my mom. The fear of "lack" nudged me to constantly work hard as a student and worker for my home. Over time, the fear of lack evolved into a fear of my family becoming homeless, so I became more driven while in college. I landed a banker job at the Royal Bank of Scotland immediately after college. This animalistic work ethic was actually a gift, and a sordid of other qualities seemed to develop along the way.

Connor: Somewhere along the way, I learned to listen better, process new information quickly, and could engage others, especially customers. I gloriously excelled at the job, and the next bank job after, because I simply outworked everyone else. In my mind, I was a UFC's greatest champion, and was truly on top of the world as a top sales leader at a large bank. I never took a day off. During those years, I was filled with a burning hunger to learn and master the required skills to do the job, like no other. And then one day while in my glory, I received a call to go to the VP's office, I walked in his office, and he handed the phone over to me as he left his office. My brother broke the news that my dad had passed away while taking a mid-day nap. I tell you I cried like a baby for the next hour. Apparently, everyone else knew, including the neighbors and my dad's favorite bartender. My dad's death made a profound impact on me. Despite decades of his struggle with the chronic fatigue syndrome, he was extremely kind, sincere, and always communicated his family, his struggle, and the burdens of life.

Connor: While on one level the fear of lack was motivation, I also think my father's death was a catalyst for deep introspection to understand the psychosis. In other words, how and why people are wired the way they are. What I later discovered was my dad had an extreme case of CFS, and should have rested way more than he did; and also had he purchased the expensive prescribed medicine, then it is very possible he may have been lived quite a bit longer. He stayed late to help us with homework, refused to use our family's money to purchase the medicine, and repaired or built everything needed in our home for more than twenty years. I was crestfallen when I discovered these facts. Also, I will say I began to realize I was feeling hollow inside, the obsession for money and wealth was weakening my sense of happiness and compassion. Yes, I was engaging others, but it was entirely to support the bank's bottom line. The hollowness crept into every thought at work, and I just felt numb with a desire to try something else.

Connor: I researched different career opportunities and decided to apply for a business manager position with a private shipping company. I guess my father's fascination and stories of fishing while a young lad somehow found a home in my mind. So, I was naturally curious about the position, company, and the business in general. After a few intense interviews, I was offered the job, but was placed on a 90-day performance condition, as part of the offer agreement. Since I liked the people, the culture, and how they were growing the business, I literally sailed through the performance review at the 90-day mark, and everyday ever since. I put my heart into my work, and the mind follows the mindset I maintain. I am the DJ of my career. Since I am at peace with my work, I feel oneness in it, and also view it as my work family. I work less hours than the first ten years and devote my time to building up others aligned with the company's expectation.

Rodney: Connor, you definitely have become the manifest image of someone who is the DJ of their career.

Connor: That is awesome to hear, my friend. Talking with you has been like a meditation class or somehow. Good positive energy. But I got to say I don't think I answered how I move the "crowd." Showing people you understand and care about them has been my greatest quality to influence my team and customers. My predecessor invoked the barking dog technique, which moves the crowd, but eventually it moves them out the door. My human-centered perspective stands in contrast to my peers in this industry that bark a lot to get what they want. I thank my dad and mom for who I am, and how I rock the crowd. One thing is I think taking long walks with a good friend can be powerful in the process of self-development and awareness.

Rodney: That is good to hear. I think you should write a book, as well. Give it some thought.

Connor: I will. Enjoy your day. Let's stay connected via Linkedin.

Rodney: I will. He tosses his newspaper in the trash bin, and quickly exits the coffee shop.

CHAPTER 10

CHESS CHAMPION IN BRYANT PARK

———

I notice Jake's is getting busier as lunchtime draws near. It is time to go. I pack up my things, and throw my backpack over my shoulder, and head out of Jake's. Since the weather is warm and fairly sunny, I decide to walk down to Bryant Park. It is a beautiful, garden-style park with a nice chill atmosphere with a ton of walkways and benches. Once I get there, I take a seat on the nearest bench, which is near Wafels & Dinges. I grab a colorful milkshake, tape down my placard, and lean back to enjoy my milkshake. I wait and wait for someone to walk over to me. While there on the bench, I can't help but think about the interesting conversations I had in Jake's. Everyone was so different, yet so focused on achieving career success. There was an energy about them as they walked up to my table.

Jessie seemed to glow with confidence, and I was so intrigued with her drive. Like a chess player, she assessed her work culture, un-coded the language of the leaders, and figured out what it would take to rise to the director-level position within a relative short amount of time. Solomon is not a DJ of his career yet, but he has the heart, drive, and awareness, so I think if he leverages his resources and change his mindset, he can do it. A short distance away, I see two deeply serious men playing a game of chess. I can feel their minds locked in battle as they intensely analyze what moves are best to make in order to advance their position in hopes of winning the game. The older player rubs his hand slightly over his beard, and squints his eye a bit before an unfortunate, fatal move. The college student playing the game is somewhat eager, and clearly sees what needs to be done to possibly win the game.

A hand is lifted slowly but deliberately as the move is executed with arrow-to-target precision. The older man sighs heavily takes a few puffs of his cigarette, and winces a bit in pain. He makes his move. The college player makes the final moves to win the game. What I know of chess is in order to win, a player needs to think about four to five moves ahead to set up the other player. Also, I was told by a good friend at work ideally your first move is about setting up your strategy properly to control the board or center of the board. The college player gives the older player a hearty pat on his shoulder and a handshake before packing up his chess board. The older player meanders over to a group that was watching the game. I get up and walk over to the college player, and break into an introduction. We exchange greetings and names.

Rodney: Nice to meet you, Devan.

Devan: Yes, the book writing project sounds interesting. I have a little time before I head back to the hotel. This is my last day in Manhattan. It has been exhilarating to explore parts of the city. I am flying back to South Africa. I have played against Ivan when he lived in South Africa four years ago. He always won. I practiced a lot over the year. Knowing he was here, I reached out to him to play a friendly game, and it feels too good to finally beat him. Yes! Victory!

Rodney: Cool. On his hooded sweatshirt, it says "University of Cape Town." What are you studying there?

Devan: I graduated about two years ago. I studied social work and so I work as a community social worker. Playing pick-up soccer games and learning my hand at chess were how I relaxed. It was a grueling time in my life, but I love where my career and life are now. I live life to the fullest!

Rodney: I know you are early in your career, but how are you managing your job? Are you the DJ of your career?

Devan: Laughs wildly. These are great questions. One of my professors is kind of like my mentor and she is so great at helping me think in the right way about things at work. I was always a good student, but it is tricky to land a good job in South Africa. It is all about who can get you in.

Rodney: Ok. I think you know a thing or two about strategy by the way you played that chess game. He chuckles.

Devan: Well, I worked on a few community-based research projects along with several professors and a few other students. I have never worked so hard in my life, but I enjoyed every moment of it. My plan was to build a great relationship with a few professors. I got to know them during their office hours and volunteered for any community research projects. I slept three to four hours a night back then. I really connected with my professors, and they were able to make introductions with the right people that led to the job I have now. Even though I graduated a few years back, I am very close with one of my professors as I have said. I guess it is like playing chess, you figure out who are the key players and what moves you can make with their help, but you need to have a clear and present focus on what is the successful outcome you seek to achieve based on the engagement with them. Because I am young and filled with so much drive and aggression, I work so hard at being patient. Patience has been a masterful teacher in my ability to know when to push forward and pull back in relationships. I think watching American western movies have helped me to learn patience. Have you seen the Clint Eastwood movie, *Pale Rider* or *For a Few Dollars More*?[7]

Rodney: Yeah, I like to watch western movies from time to time. I haven't seen *Pale Rider*, but I saw *For a Few Dollars More* a few times. It is a great movie about patience and timing. I literally loved how they used the pocket watch to draw the intensity of action around the gunfights. It was so interesting.

Devan: Exactly. Remember, the final gunfight scene in the movie between Eastwood as *The Man with No Name*[8] and El Indio, the beauty of that gun fight was each fighter was timing when to shoot based on when the chime song of the pocket watch would stop. When the pocket watch was about to stop the music, Van Clef walks in with another pocket watch playing the same

---

7   *Pale Rider*, directed by Clint Eastwood and Linnie Niehaus (1985: Burbank, CA: Warner Home Video 1991), DVD.

8   *For a Few Dollars More*, directed by Sergio Leone (1965, Italy: MGM Home Entertainment 1998), DVD.

song, which distracted El Indio, and Eastwood was perfectly in control of his emotions and reacted precisely at the right time to shoot and kill El Indio. As I think back, I think El Indio would have won because his instinct and reaction were set to respond based on the illusion of control he had in winning so many other gunfights by totally distracting and confusing his opponents with the playing the chime song, but Van Clef and Eastwood distracted his mind and emotions, so he reacted a split second slower, and therefore, he did not win. I think I am the DJ of my career because I know how to position myself for victory with extremely well-timed action steps that move me closely to what I am seeking. I ask my mentors lots of questions all the time, and try to understand how they think, and apply their advice as often as I can. It is not enough to work for something you want, I think it is more important to know what steps should be taken and who can help you along the way.

Rodney: Man, I never thought of things that way, especially the way in which you described the final gunfight scene. That is cool.

Devan: Yeah, I know I can get kind of deep on this stuff. It is I really think the focus on timing can create a powerful, strategic position or can be used deceptively to mislead your opponent to take a particular course of direction—I do that whenever I play chess, work, or play a pick-up game of soccer. In order to win a long game in anything, I think timing and patience needs to be part of anything you want. Rodney, I better get going. I need to grab a quick lunch before heading back to the hotel.

Rodney: Okay. It was great talking with you. I will reach out to you once the book is done. Have a safe flight to South Africa. Victory! We shake hands before I walk off.

CHAPTER 11

THE WIZARD OF OZ

———

I walk back to the Moxy Hotel. When I get back to my room, I fall into a deep sleep. I meet up with my friend, Helena, for dinner in my hotel's restaurant, and we catch a subway over to the Saint James Hotel in Tribeca. On Friday nights, they have an amazing DJ who rips some amazing old and new rap music. There is no cover, but you are escorted to the roof top lounge by the doorman, at least, he rode up with us. He was cool and funny, so it was an entertaining ride to the top floor. As the elevator doors open, the music is intoxicating, fills the air with a hypnotic, pulsating beat. We take a seat on a long sofa near a fireplace across the dance floor. The DJ flows through an epic set of mixes, fist pointing, and playfully smiling at everyone moving or nodding to his DJ magic, as he seemingly plays ever-deeper, twisted, harmonized mixed songs with a uncanny instinct to phase in rap hooks from Biggie Smalls, Jay-Z, and Lady Gaga. The DJ rules, controls, and turns up the volume of our energy, dance, and kindred laughter in the repeating moments of excitement, intoxication, and euphoria we feel. When the DJ takes a break to grab a drink while he plays the long version of KRS' *Sparkin Madizms*, I seize the moment, and ask him, "what makes you the Wizard of Oz?"

DJ: Really, I am the little white midget in the big fancy castle while eating free fried chicken? Okay, I can do that.

Rodney: You are slaying the music on the wheels of steel in your power box. So, you are the Wizard.

DJ: It is just I want to blow their mind in ways they have never dreamed of. I got to make the ladies dance, and it flows from there.

Rodney: So, you are a creative genius wizard who eats the free chicken.

DJ: You got it, my man.

We fist bump, and he heads back to multi-color gyrating DJ platform and changes up the synthesizes a new mix of beats for the music hungry crowd. I grab two mixed drinks before heading back to the sofa.

Rodney: Helena, what makes a DJ good at what they do? I mean, what does a really, really great DJ do the average DJ doesn't? I know you've been to like about a hundred rooftop lounges, dance parties, and birthday parties with a live DJ.

Helena: Yeah, you are probably right. Well, some DJs are good when they know how to move the crowd, teases with all sorts of mixes, builds the energy, and just flows with amazing vibes. I like to be absorbed into the flow. You can feel it.

Rodney: So, they are like anyone who is great at what they do whether a nurse, engineer, teacher, or business consultant—so long as they understand the customer, mastered their core skills, knows how to persuade, knows how to build emotional connection, and just flows with positive gravitas. You can feel it and want to be around it. Is that true?

Helena: Okay, but if the professional knows their stuff, then they need to be able to turn it on like a snap of their fingers. For anyone good at what they do, it should look natural and show quickly.

Rodney: Like Neo from the *Matrix*[9] after he discovered his abilities?

Helena: Yeah, but not when he beat Morpheus. He had the power only after he challenged the agent on the roof of the skyscraper. Check out the bartender over there. He is really screwing up the drinks. He doesn't know what he is doing, cause I had to repeat my order too many times, and he could not find the right liquor bottles to make the damn drink I wanted. I wish Neo were here to beat his ass and make me the right drink.

Rodney: LOL. You are funny, but I get your point. We order another round of drinks and enjoy the music for a few more hours.

---

9   *The Matrix*, directed by Andy Wachowski and Larry Wachowski, (1999: Burbank, CA: Warner Bros. Pictures, 1999), DVD.

CHAPTER 12

STREET CONVERSATIONS IN NYC

The next morning, I grab a large green tea at the café next to the Moxy Hotel's entrance. I begin to randomly walk to the heart of Times Square. I notice a cluster of superhero characters crowded around a large group of tourists, so I cross over to the other side of the street to stay clear of the mob. Spiderman and Elmo look disappointed, but I keep up my pace as I begin my trek to Central Park. I figure I can just dive into some street conversations with strangers in in the park. Since my outing at Bryant Park was so good, why not try my luck at one of the largest parks in New York City.

I notice a couple wearing identical Brazilian National Football shirts walking towards the bicycle stand.

I say, "hey nice shirts, and what a fantastic team." They turn, smile, and the man says his English is not good. I smile politely and walk pass them. There is a young woman leaning against a tree. As I approach, I see her friend standing somewhat close to her is nervously looking at me as I approach, so I abort my interest in a conversation and turn to walk down a major walkway into the park. Feeling kind of awkward, but I am not discouraged.

A man dressed in Tibetan clothing offers a small, braided colorful bracelet for a donation. I give him a $5 dollar bill and say, "you are like a sunshine" as I nod, then take the bracelet and walkaway. As I look back, I see he takes a $10 dollar bill from the hand of a zookeeper. The Central Park Zoo is embroidered on his shirt sleeve. I strike up a conversation with him.

Rodney: Hi, I notice you are a zookeeper.

Zoo Cleaner: No, I just clean the catches and help out around the zoo.

Rodney: My name is Rodney. I am from Washington, DC, and am writing my first book. I am here to have random conversations with people about managing their careers.

Zoo Cleaner: That's cool. My name is Ted. I work at the zoo part-time and work tables at night.

I tell Ted about why I am writing this book and the rationale behind the title. He nods with a big smile, leans over, and says my girl would be the most perfect person to interview. Ted was walking three steps faster than me because he was about five minutes away from the zoo's entrance, and his shift was starting in ten minutes. Ted is in his early twenties but had a beard longer than mine. During our brief conversation, I learned Ted's girlfriend, Sarita, was an aspiring screenwriter and also worked tables at the same restaurant with him. Despite my shaky hands, I manage to type her name and number into my phone while Ted sends her a text message. Ted says she is super cool for an older lady. He chuckles, shakes my hand, and runs toward to the zoo's entrance.

I shoot Sarita a text message, and she responds a second later. She wants to know if her roommate can be interviewed as well. We agree to meet at a Starbucks Coffee up the street from her loft. I arrive early, nab three chairs at a long window table, and get comfortable while waiting for them.

Warning to all aspiring writers, a Starbucks Coffee shop anywhere in NYC is not an ideal place to interview anyone. I offered to buy a musician a cup of coffee, because he actually was cratered deeply in one of the chairs near the long window table. He spouts I was leaving anyway as he practically snatches the large mocha vente from my hands. If he was so cool with giving up his chair, then why all the attitude when he gave up his chair. I hope that he is reading this. Dude, you were rude... next time, just say no if you don't want to give up your spot in a Starbucks. I am just saying.

I get a text from Sarita and her friend letting me know they are entering the Starbucks Coffee, and I tell her where I am sitting. She is riding a cloud of laughter as she, and her roomie walk over to me. Oh my gosh, she has a big personality. She high fives two coffee baristas and throws a straw at a co-worker head down in a romance novel. I like her style.

Sarita: Rodney! She sings, "Hey, Mr. DJ won't play that song for me all night, all night long..." The friend twirls and pretends to demonstrate the early 90s dance called the running man. I shed tears of laughter.

Connie: Hi. I am Curious Connie. I am intrigued by this little project I had to crash the party.

Rodney: You and you are very funny. Pointing at each of them with a playful smile.

Sarita: I am Ike, and she is Tina.

Connie: Bitch, please. I am Salt and you are Peppa. I know she said "Peppa," but she meant "Pepper," I guess. In my mind, I say please don't change careers, and just stay in photography.

Rodney: The female rap group?

Connie: Nope, the spices. Ain't that nice?

Rodney: I smile. Are you sure you don't want to pursue a career as stand-up comedians?

Sarita: I tried all that. Now, I am pursuing my teaching degree, and plan to become a high school English teacher. Before you come at me with your DJ questions, I want you to know I am the DJ of my career, ruler of my destiny, and I am enlisting my army of friends to help me be true to myself. As the saying goes, "to thine own self be true."

Connie: Amen, sister.

Rodney: So, you are not a screenwriter? Connie, what do you do?

Sarita: Ted never gets it right. Now, you can understand why he is not a zookeeper, right? He is a good roommate, though. Connie is a photographer, and a brand ambassador.

Rodney: I don't ask Sarita about her relationship with Ted but go straight to the questions since I know they got places to be, people to see, and all that jazz. When did you know you wanted to do what you do in your career?

Connie: I was always fascinated with trying to capture a great moment through the photographic lens. The happiness, joy, and beauty of the moment in photography, film, or art channels all the feelings that make me feel alive, vulnerable, and strong, if that makes sense. I always had a camera in my hand as a teenager, and actually have a picture of having sex with my first girlfriend. That pic is a keeper!

Sarita: Yep, that pic is a keeper. I have seen it, hot beauty caught in a moment of ecstasy. Mr. DJ, don't worry, this interview is not going to get slapped with a NC-17 rating. We can keep it PG-13 for your readers.

Rodney: Say whatever is real for you. This is your story, boo. She smiles too much after I say that.

Sarita: I thought I wanted to be a screenwriter and filmmaker, but after talking with many people in that profession I realized I didn't want to fight that hard for a career where women are given far less opportunity for success than a man. I know I could have been a trailblazer, but I need to pay my bills and rent is too damn high, so I figure I could enjoy a career as a teacher for a little bit more pay, and pick up a few writing gigs on the side. I want to write screenplays, of course, but I can do so as a secondary job. I love the idea of educating, shaping, and inspiring young minds. I think being a teacher is my calling because I have always admired, been entertained, and inspired by them. So, yes, that is what I want to do. It is me, boo.

Rodney: Who are the influencers, mentors, and sources of inspiration in your life?

Connie: Wow, you really packed it in that question. It sounds like that should have been two or three separate questions. I am just saying.

Sarita: I feel you, Connie. But I like this question. It is all tied together. Give me a second to think about it. Well, I think Malcolm the concierge of our apartment is a mentor and influencer. I see Sarita's eyes grow a bit larger as she talks, and her pauses anchor the words she expresses. He is retired from the US Navy, donates to four charities, volunteers at the Boys and Girls Club, and has worked in our building for the last fifteen years. He takes time to get to know everyone in the building, shares life advice, and is always reading a new book. I didn't know until last week he is blind in his left eye.

As her voice cracks for the first time, I hear the voice of a girl who is trying to find a stronger voice while talking about someone she admires. In my life, I have puffed up to sound strong to impress or be cool, to only be deflated by the prickly reality I am drawing strength from weakness is no different than a young teenager pretending to be an adult, so I resolved to be honest, authentic, and present to the circumstance. I shift back to listen to Sarita.

Sarita: When I asked him about his blind eye, he said it was God's gift. When walking down the hallway to my apartment that day something started to move inside and found its way to the windows of my eyes, I couldn't stop the well of tears flowing down my face as I looked in the mirror. I know I am physically attractive by the obvious reaction of others, but in that reflecting moment I felt ugly and selfish inside. Because of Malcolm, I have started volunteering at a women's shelter and discovered a new person inside of me. I see meaning and beauty in giving one's time to help others in need. Honestly, I think over the last four years of living in my apartment building, I think the conversations with Malcolm even changed my career direction.

Sarita: Also, I think my church-going catholic mom has been a dramatic influence in my life over the last few years. It is just her words are so full of freaking love, and sincerity in helping me to avoid developing bad habits and making the wrong choices. I have made a ton of mistakes in my early twenties, but I think living a stone's throw away from Central Park and having the best roomies in the world has changed me for the better. I love people watching and thinking about the lives of people when walking around Central Park. I want to become a teacher because I need to help these kids learn how to understand their voice and express it in a way people will listen and truly hear them. The last thing I want to say is I am inspired by great courage. There are a lot of people who have great ideas and great minds, but significant acts of courage really move me. Anyone can be confident if they look good, talk good, and the world says they think good, but courage is something extraordinary that defines character and strength more than anything else in my opinion.

Connie: Ditto. I totally agree with you about Malcolm. He is an incredible human being with great courage and sacrifice for others. My younger sister is my greatest inspiration. She was hit by a car when she was eleven years old. I choke a bit on my drink as Connie shares her pain, admiration, and love for her little sister. I think back to my grandmother and her constant smile, even in the face of failing health and the onslaught of endless bad news from her doctors. A smile that was stronger than an oak tree—alive with happiness, love, and endless commitment to inspire and brighten the lives of her grandchildren, sons, and daughters. I am transfixed on this moment as it hangs in the air. I look deep in the eyes of Connie to see that her words continue to move slower and heavy. She can't walk, she can't walk... she can't walk, and her motor skills are still off. But, over the last year, I am shocked to say she is teaching her body to walk again. I don't go to church, but I think her prayers and meditation have played a massive impact on what is happening to her. I am not sure if she will be able to fully walk, but she can pull herself out of the wheelchair and can take ten steps on her own.

Connie begins to cry for a long time. We all shed tears, and I look over to see the coffee baristas shedding tears, too. This moment is surreal and emotionally powerful.

We spend the next hour talking with Connie about her sister. She shares pictures of her family and talks more about her sister. We close out the interview with them trying to sing old school rap songs. I spent three hours in conversation, and only about forty-five minutes interviewing them, but what was shared was enough to write two books.

We hug and say goodbyes. I walk back to the Moxy and pack up for my early morning bus ride back to Washington, DC. I am on sensory overload after experiencing so many great conversations and experiences in NYC. I need to decompress, reflect, and I am looking forward to the bus ride home.

CHAPTER 13

MARY KITSON

———

Finally! After many failed attempts, I am finally able to reach Mary Kitson, a senior-level program manager who skillfully manages organization development, change management, planning, and workforce strategy, for a large not-for-profit organization that specializes in federally funded research and development initiatives. She is the "Anthony Bourdain" of her craft at her company—brimming with engaging and positive energy built on the foundation of brilliance, a deep sense of curiosity and morality. Like Bourdain, she is an extraordinary student of learning, appreciates a great wine, and possesses hawk-eyed clarity in how to articulate the process of learning for individuals, teams, and leaders through a common language that inspires an open-mind, introspection, and a decision to take action.

If working ten-hour days was not enough, Mary created the Society of Human Resource Management (SHRM) Mentor HR Program for HR professionals in the Washington, DC metro area twenty years ago. She directs the activities of the twenty-person subject matter expert volunteer team for this nationally recognized mentoring, personal leadership development, and professional networking organization with over 500 alumni and fourteen new members for each cohort annually.

The breadth and scope of this mentoring and leadership development program is amazing. Having completed this program personally, I am extremely grateful for this opportunity to interview this leader about her career and share the pearls of wisdom she can share with others.

We agree to a Saturday afternoon conversation.

Rodney: Good morning, Mary.

Mary: Good morning. I had a conversation last night with some of the members of your cohort. They were excited to hear you are taking the plunge to write a book about a topic that is so important to you.

Rodney: That is great to hear! I always enjoyed my cohort class. Let me say I appreciate your taking time out of your busy schedule to share your career story.

Mary: Before we begin, who is the book's audience? I am curious.

Rodney: Well, I initially had thought it would be for recent college graduates. But, after interviewing people, I think the audience is really anyone needing career inspiration or needing to know what it takes to be successful in growing and managing their career.

Mary: Okay, cool. I am curious about the audience you had in mind.

Rodney: Feel free to ask any questions. Curiosity is a good thing. Since I want to be respectful to the time you have given me, I better dive into my questions. Right off the bat, I was wondering how did you figure out or discover what career path was best for you?

Mary: Three words: mentors, mentors, mentors. They were extremely helpful in college as I was trying to navigate the direction of my life. At my core, I have always been interested in making a difference in others' lives and helping them to solve problems. I think I was the age of six when I realized that.

Hmm...age six? That's amazing. At that age, I was more interested in how I could meet Cookie Monster and Big Bird from Sesame Street than any altruistic need to help others. I wonder how much her parents and friends influenced her concern for others. I admire how this behavioral value was nurtured and evolved in her professional life.

A lot of my roles, whether volunteering or early jobs, always seemed to be at the intersection of the three-legged stool— that is, people, process, and technology. I'm like the glue that holds the structure together and keeps it functional. I started out as an accounting major in college before making the change to business management. During my college years, I was fortunate. I was surrounded by a supportive network of friends and professors. In fact, because of my involvement in campus activities, I developed a close relationship with a few of the resident advisers, who shared excellent advice that helped me to form my thoughts on what type of career I wanted to pursue after college.

Rodney: What was your first professional job?

Mary: I landed a job as a technical recruiter at a large environmental consulting firm for two years and left that position to become a recruiting manager for a 1,000-person engineering firm. I worked there for a few years before returning to graduate school to pursue a Master's degree in Human Resource Development. I transitioned into management consulting and worked at two for-profit companies before joining a non-profit think tank which allowed me to work on both management and technology consulting at the edge of innovation. This work is perfect for my interest in playing at the intersection of the proverbial three-legged stool, and I quickly became absorbed in teaching executives and other senior level government staff how to navigate the paradigm shift of change.

Rodney: To roll back time a bit, who or what has been the greatest influence on your professional life?

Mary: Again, I would say my mentors. I have a spiderweb-like network of mentors on two levels: peer-level leaders that I met and still work with in some capacity through my SHRM Mentor HR Program, and those who are more senior on the organizational hierarchy who serve as my advocates at work. My peer mentors help to sanity-check and test my ideas before I take action, and they serve as a sounding board and provide strategic feedback. My advocates are a range of senior-level to executive-level staff at work who know my reputation and believe in the direction I want to guide the programs and projects I lead. The nature of the trust relationship is really key. What I have found is cultivating mutually beneficial relationships and helping each other to move forward on initiatives of shared importance is like planting a seed and nurturing it. I have also been lucky that one of my best advocates at work selected me to backfill her for a couple of assignments when she was ready to move on to her next gig. I didn't always feel like I was ready, however she pushed me and believed in my abilities.

Rodney: What is the source of your motivation to succeed?

Mary: My desire to be a leader. I often create my own roles. I start by asking curious questions about why something is the way it is and if there is a desire to do something different. Then I help people design a new, better way forward. I'm not afraid to respectfully challenge executives or raise provocative issues others don't feel comfortable with. I often fulfill the role of helping others to get unstuck, and I think carefully about what is important to these individuals and take action on their behalf to move things forward with and for them.

Rodney: What advice would you give to a classroom of college seniors about how to deal with a failure?

Mary: I am super interested in design thinking right now, so that is my frame of reference. I would tell them to hold the view of failure as an experiment, own what happened, learn from the situation, and design your way forward. Do not dwell on the feeling of failure, nor let it define you. We all make mistakes, and it is how you react to it is most important. Use it as part of your personal story of how you learn and recover stronger than before. In design thinking, there is no such thing as a failure. You apply what you learn to brainstorming and constructing prototypes. It is also healthy to practice the law of de-attachment, meaning to give up your attachment to a specific outcome, and focus more on the journey. I have learned meditation or taking a mindful walk is recharging and allows you to engage from a fresher perspective.

Rodney: What have you learned about managing your career? What advice would you give to your early career self?

Mary: I am in charge of my career, and no one is going to do it for me. It is really about what you want and what is important to you. I often look for gaps that may exist in the organization I work for, and where can I create an opportunity in that white space. It's important to know your values and strengths. Ask yourself what you want out of your career? How coherent is that with your life view? Do you experience any conflict between the two? Be mindful as your life changes and evolves you may want different things out of your career. 360-degree assessments and different mentors have helped me to become more aware of my blind spots. Sometimes we need trusted advisors to help us see if we are behaving in a way that is consistent with how we want others to see us. Are your words, actions, and thoughts aligned?

Rodney: If suddenly one of your strongest skills became unusable, how would you make up for that lack of specific skills, and/or develop your existing skills to maintain your same level of performance? For example, if you suddenly developed a severe case of laryngitis, and as a result your clarion gift of persuasive verbal communication was unusable for a few months.

Mary: Several months ago, I had a serious concussion which caused vision problems and a loss of my ability to concentrate and analyze information. I was unable to perform many of the functions of my job. It was incredibly scary and I began to wonder if I needed to find a new career. People would ask me a series of analytical questions in a noisy meeting room and that was overwhelming. I simply couldn't process information like I could before my concussion. No more multi-tasking!

Mary: To answer your question more specifically, I was asked to prepare and present a twenty-page technical report. You can't imagine how difficult this report became for me. It took about three to four times the amount of time to complete it. I was able to use the creative part of my brain, while my analytical brain was in hibernation. I ended up convincing some colleagues to help me brainstorm ideas and then I applied more of a reporting on the results of an experiment to the paper. It allowed me to use more of a creative approach. Having the courage to push forward in the face of adversity and shifting my mindset were absolutely critical to pull this off. It might not have been my best work; however, I delivered the product on time.

Rodney: How do you develop your current skills? In other words, how you do you improve your existing skills?

Mary: I stay on top of trends, innovation, and leap ahead thinking. I read articles, listen to podcasts, and attend professional conferences. I like to talk with others in different organizations about how they are approaching similar problems and issues. I like to take on new assignments where I have an opportunity to stretch my skills. I rely heavily on my network to find out about internal job leads.

Rodney: How do you learn? What have been the best professional sources for learning? For example, I love comic improv class, and have learned a lot about myself from that. Most people tend to give polite feedback, but only share deep feedback when the stakes are high.

Mary: Deeper learning helps me to reflect on any adjustments I need to make to my behavior or values system. I need to create both the physical and mental space for that to happen. Two years ago, I completed a leadership coaching certificate program, which ultimately helped me to be a better listener, teacher, leader. I now approach things from a more curious, non-judgmental perspective. I had to carve out the space in my priority-overloaded schedule and I had to create the open space in my mind. It was an important commitment for me to make, however, I had to make tradeoffs with other activities in my life. Additionally, I go on a personal leadership retreat a couple times of a year. I often take weekend or week-long meditation workshops at the Omega Institute for Holistic Studies in the Hudson Valley of New York. Last summer I discovered how much I love Tara Brach's teachings. Meditation has been a transformational practice for me. In the midst of crisis or particularly stressful situation I am (usually) able to pause, breathe, and manage my emotions. As a leader, this emotional balance is particularly important, so I am showing up for others in the way they need me to.

Rodney: In the DJ world, the critical achievement in persuading your customers, aka the crowd, is to get them dancing or moving to the music. How do you achieve persuasion in positively influencing your customers or the crowd?

Mary: I like to find out what is important to people and what their pain points are. I think about their likely position on an issue and I design solutions with that in mind or convey tradeoffs to them in a way that acknowledges what I know is important. One of my top strengths in Clifton Strengths terms, is Individualization, which means I am intrigued with the unique qualities of each person and naturally figure out how people who are different can work together productively. I am like a casting director, using what I know about people to influence them to take a particular action or make a certain type of decision.

Rodney: How do you obtain the "real" feedback that you need to grow?

Mary: Just ask others for it. Ask what you did well and less well on a project. Asking for feedback requires that you need to be open to what you hear and set your ego aside. Consider taking a 360-degree feedback assessment, reflect on what you hear, and commit to implementing an action plan. Sometimes, I'll ask people on my team how well I am serving their needs and if I need to adjust anything. It's important to create a safe space for that conversation to happen or people won't share.

Rodney: Are you the DJ of your career? How do you know?

Mary: Yes! I help people to spin ideas and unleash their potential in the world. When I am doing this, I am engaged, energized, and in the state of flow. Being in a state of flow is this highly focused mental state where you are not even thinking about the task at hand, you're just doing it and feeling joy.

CHAPTER 14

PEOPLE OF THE EARTH

———

About three months ago, I was in the audience at the Kennedy Performing Arts Center in Washington, DC, and I was mesmerized by a mix of Cuban and neo soul music from the People of the Earth. It was a packed audience, but I managed to get a spot to see this large band bring their music to the stage. Gabriel is the brilliant and talented founder and leader of the band. It is a good thing his band had a Facebook page, so I sent a message to contact him. A few days later he responded to arrange for a conversation.

Rodney: Hi Gabriel, thank you for being available for this conversation. I think your band's performance at the Kennedy Center was incredibly beautiful and engaging. The energy was amazing! Tell me about your band.

Gabriel: People of Earth is a global music collective set on blurring the barriers between the great art forms of the terrestrial sphere, creating an explosive blend of the music of Cuba, Puerto Rico, Brazil and beyond. We are a fourteen-band with eight nationalities with a passion for creating a chemistry of music that represents who we are and what we like. I am the Director and formed the band years ago.

Rodney: Cool. Tell me about you and how you formed the band.

Gabriel: I have always been fascinated with music from classical, jazz (all types), Latin, and Cuban. As a student at the Curtis Institute of Music in Philadelphia, I studied classical, and my musical interests evolved from there. I am a percussionist, composer, and educator. I moved to New York City in 2012. It was a great year for me. I dove deeper into discovering the city, and kind of exploded in my love for Cuban dance music. A year later, I felt I was ready to start a band, and it totally failed to get off the ground. None of us had the expertise to form the Cuban music we wanted to play. The band fell apart.

Rodney: What did you do after it failed? Did you try again?

Gabriel: After the band fell apart, I went to Cuba to become a student again to really learn the culture, build relationships with great musicians (from the street corner musician to some local greats), food, and history. Because of my love for people and the art of music, I was introduced to so many people, and learned from brilliantly passionate and gifted musical masters. In Cuba, music is all around you. I saw music in the eyes, smiles, and everyday movement of people. I left Cuba ready to return to New York City to start over. I didn't leave alone. I invited one of talented Cuban musicians to move to New York with me. And thankfully, Keisel, agreed to go.

Rodney: Why did you decide to bring Keisel with you?

Gabriel: We connected as musicians and friends. He has played in over one hundred countries. Keisel is a master percussionist and is incredibly knowledgeable about different styles of Cuban music. The guy is brilliant, improvises, and can naturally flow—even if there is a last-minute change in songs that need to be played. Basically, we had a lot in common, and he was interested in starting a new life in New York City. So, I helped him to become an educator, and become one of my roommates.

Rodney: That's cool. Tell me about how you develop your skills? How do you get better at what you do?

Gabriel: The world I am in as a musician is very competitive. My audience can be very loyal, but if I don't constantly improve or fail to perform at my highest level, I could lose them. So, because I have an understanding of my skills, how musical instruments should be played, and how to connect with the audience, it is critical to practice, practice, and practice again. I reach out to my band members to work on our craft, learn new ways of playing, and experimenting with things. Through practice and constant communication on what sounds good, I/we improve. Recording myself and observing how the audience responds whenever we play a gig is a teaching moment. I think it is so important to learn and improve from those teaching moments. Sometimes, I learn more from failing—when the audience doesn't respond positively or simply is not into the energy of the song—than from a successful gig. As a band, we've learned how to give and take feedback, and grow from it.

Rodney: How do you stay focused?

Gabriel: I think my drive to perform the best music for every person that listens to us at a live event is what keeps my mind in the right place. Also, whenever I read a positive comment from my fans on social media sites really gets to me. Of course, the synergy between my band members keeps us on point, too.

Rodney: How important is networking and building relationships to you?

Gabriel: Everyone in every profession needs to be constantly building relationships and getting to know people. You can have a job today, and then it can be gone tomorrow. There is nothing in life that is promised. I wish I had started relationship-building earlier. I have maintained some good relationships from college, but I should have done more of it. We truly reap what we sow as far as getting to know others. As a musician whose music is embraced by so many different types of people, I have learned to figure out how to communicate with a variety of people. When you can talk with different types of people, there is possibility you can grow your network, and therefore your gigs with a wider spectrum of diverse people. I find it so exciting as the band's leader, I am helping others to become invested in what we do. Our fans buy t-shirts, track us on social media, buy the music, and pay to see us live. To borrow your book's title, I believe I am the DJ of my career.

Rodney: Gabriel, what would you tell anyone who is wanting to be the DJ of their career?

Gabriel: Invest your skills, knowledge, and people. With competition so strong in every field because of technology and globalism, I think it is critical to develop skills and knowledge and keep pushing yourself to a higher level. Also, I have invested in the success of others. It doesn't have to be money, it could be sharing your knowledge, sharing your skills, and taking time to inspire someone.

Rodney: Thank you for what you have shared about you and your band. Enjoy the rest of your day. We mutually end the phone call.

I am seeing stars after the conversation with Gabriel. Everything he said made perfect sense regarding how to manage one's career and his passion for learning how to be a better musician and leader. Working extremely hard and recognizing how to improve the skills of others in his band is incredible. He invests every fiber of his being into his band's success. This all or nothing approach is a testament to his deep belief and commitment to his art. I could feel his mind, body, and spirit are unified in his commitment. So, I suppose one critical element in career success is a commitment to continuous awareness and consistent investment in one's skills for the challenge of the stage or office at any given moment. I have much work to do in myself on this area.

CHAPTER 15

CONVERSATION WITH A NATIONAL MARKETING MANAGER

Rodney: What comes to mind when I say, "Be the DJ of Your Career." What does it mean to you? What thoughts come to mind?

Janice: I really like this declarative statement. It is like saying "stand strong and be the owner of your career despite the crazy shit you will need to deal with along the way." The small voice in my head says like I got a choice anyway so be the damn DJ of your career and succeed at work! It is empowering, I love it! Having been on the receiving end of three layoffs, seven contract jobs, and four bad bosses, it is incredibly hard to feel like we can be the "DJ" of our own careers in today's workforce. I mean there are so many dynamics at play, including the looming threat of robots and artificial intelligence taking your job. But I think deeply one needs to build a network of influential people and constantly take their skills to the next level in a purposed-driven way... there is power in that. I feel more confident, powerful, and self-aware than I have ever been at any point in my career.

Rodney: Cool. Why do you believe it is important to feel the way you feel about yourself in your profession? I mean, you could be called into the bosses' office tomorrow to receive a pink slip.

Janice: The power of anyone doesn't rest in what job you have, but rather in the knowledge you are on top of your game or are on the path to being the best. I guess it is always feeling that you are the "chosen one."

Rodney: Chosen one? Like Eddie Murphy was the chosen one in *The Golden Child.* So, are you saying that feeling that every moment in every day at work you are the "chosen one" or on a chosen path to incredible career success is important?

Janice: I think feeling like the chosen one fills me with a deep sense that my life's career purpose involves happiness, believing I should feel deeply engaged, and called to impact the lives of my direct reports, leadership, and customers in a positively transformative way. I think it is more than being selected to have a special gift.

Rodney: That is interesting. As I reflect on a few conversations I have had with others on this, there is not a common thread, which I had presumed, I think it is a rather personal journey of discovery, self-awareness, and inner drive or hunger to rise and live a great work life.

Janice: I guess a great DJ becomes great over time, but the little things they do a million times with so much self-belief fills the DJ with confidence, I suppose. Yeah, same here for me, I never was a good student in college. I worked twice as hard as my other classmates, and even in the professional world, I was literally slow at learning the right skills for my job until something clicked in my mind, and I became more focused and my drive for success intensified. I think failing my team on my second job was a pivotal experience. Some mistakes are forgiven, but others can be devastating.

Rodney: I see. So, you think great DJs, and professionals alike, are created more often than a burning desire of hunger to be incredibly successful for themselves, for a team, or someone close to them?

Janice: Yes, I think there is someone or something that drives them to believe they need to be the best. I don't think it stops at just performing at a high level. I think it evolves into a state of mind in order to maintain success in what they do. For example, while I am always pushing myself, I naturally push others to be their best version of themselves around me, including my boss. I don't settle on what is status quo, I think there is a constant push and pull in regards to mentally and physically perceive that one is the king of the mountain at work. It is constantly looking at any feedback, actual work results, and analyzing how to increase a more positive perception over our peers.

Rodney: How do you recharge?

Janice: I do things to reduce stress: travel to Miami, eat healthy, maintain a positive mind, and get a good night's sleep every night. I come from a large family with many extended relatives. I host family barbeques and go to a ton of birthday parties.

Rodney: What advice would you give to anyone seeking to Be the DJ of their career?

Janice: Damn. Didn't you already ask me this question? Just kidding. I know why the caged bird sings, and I certainly know what it takes for anyone to be the DJ of their career. One must know who they are as a human being, how to access their skill development, and execute daily on a plan to grow your skills, grow your professional relationships, and grow your ability to sense bullshit (self is not excluded). That's it. That's what I believe it takes.

CHAPTER 16

CONVERSATION WITH THE SUGAR CANE MAN

—

Rodney: Hi Tomas.

Tomas: Good morning sir. I mowed the front and back yard. Do you need basement steps cleaned? Also, I can trim the hedges.

Rodney: I can do that myself. How long have you been a landscaper?

Tomas: Brotha, I work part-time at this. My wife cleans houses. I retired from custodial work for the city about two years ago.

Rodney: How many years did you work as a custodian in DC?

Tomas: Whew... it was twenty-three years, but I worked in sugar cane fields all over Florida for fifteen years. When I lived in Panama, my dad and mom owned a small farm and were fruit peddlers. There is nothing more beautiful than picking fruit from our trees in the early morning, nothing sweeter than watermelon, and nothing tastes as good as fried chicken with yam.

Rodney: What have you learned about working in America?

Tomas: Life here is hard. People are nice, but sometimes don't like you. A friend helped me to get my job as a custodian. I worked alone and did what the boss said. I had four bosses over twenty-three years. I loved the first three, but it was a struggle to work for the last boss. He was a mean person and always called me on my day off to help out. I said "no" a few times, and he got upset. I never called out sick either. Young people today don't want to work hard and quit when shit makes them mad. Everybody quit when they are not happy. No matter how tired you are, no matter how hard the work is, you must keep working. Sometimes, things were terrible for us, but we never gave up. I moved three times because the rent was too damn high.

Rodney: You and your wife raised five kids?

Tomas: Yes. We never gave up. I was always tired. I am tired now, but I keep working. It is good for your head. Don't hurt your freaking head. If you work, you will stay strong and happy. God blesses a hardworking family.

Rodney: What do you tell your oldest daughter in nursing school?

Tomas: She is a fighter. Sandra always work hard, and never give up. She has some school loans. She went to community college, and now she is in her last year. We pray for her a lot. Sandra is our hero. She does everything for the family. She remembers her grandma and grandpa. I think when you do things for other people it will make you stronger so you can fight harder.

The squint of his eye is a window into the sacrifices to help his daughter. I can feel the love and hope that overflows from every word he shares about her. Tomas slightly shakes his fist as he emphasizes, she is a fighter, and so is he. Tomas chokes a bit on the pain of knowing his daughter works phenomenally hard. I remember not too long ago when I was a college student needing to work part-time, and the exhaustingly long walks home after a day of class and work. It was too expensive to live in a student dorm and so I saved money by living at home.

Rodney: I hear you. So, are you saying people today need to work harder, never give up, and help each other? Tomas, I think it is harder today, because of so many things, and people are tricky to work for.

Tomas: I know. My youngest son cannot work with people. He is not as fast as Sandra. He needs to work alone. I pray he can find a custodian job. I think all these movies and bad friends can mess with a young person's mind.

Rodney: What would you tell anyone who is trying to do good in their job?

Tomas: My grandpa told my dad, and my dad told me, and I tell my children they and all of us [referring to his family] must live to give to the next generation. Take a little job and become the best at what you do. I worked for a long-time cutting, stripping off leaves, and we put the sugar cane in a wheelie to take it away. You know, sometimes, I talk to the sugar cane, to help it know it needs to be soft for me to cut. I tell it if it is too hard, no one can eat you. I believe you need to talk to your work, to make things better. I look at Tomas like he is crazy. We both laugh.

Tomas: When the sugar cane season ends in fall, I helped with mowing, cutting hedges, and clean houses, too. My son and every person working must learn how to be the best, learn how to work with all types of people, and learn how to laugh at work. I laugh all the time, and my wife makes me laugh in the bed. We both laugh again.

Rodney: I pray your son can find a good job, too. I pay Tomas in cash. I give him a fist bump before he walks over to my neighbor's house.

CHAPTER 17

WHAT I WOULD TELL MY YOUNGER SELF

There is so much I would say to my younger self in effort to be the DJ of my career. I feel very fortunate that I have had some great things happened in my career, but I have also made some major mistakes, and there have been so many failures that I have lost count. Looking back, I honestly think if my older self could have been a voice in my head, I would have made significantly wiser decisions, impacted the lives of others more positively, and generally been more centered in my being.

KNOW YOUR SKILLS

As I reflect on the interviews I had in preparation for writing this book, I think this bit of wisdom is the most important. Please take time to figure out what are your skills. In other words, let your mind wander about the things people would be willing to pay for you to do—and I am not talking about illegal stuff. Yeah, I know that is not saying enough about what I mean by that. What are things your parents, your teachers, and friends have said you are good at. (Remember when Morpheus said to Neo in *The Matrix*[10], "I know you're better than this. Why are you holding back? Set your mind free." He understood Neo was "the one" and he had a particular set of extraordinary abilities that could help his team in the fight against the Agent). Now if you don't have a Morpheus in your life, what are your areas of interest and hobbies? There is always more runway in your path of career discovery than you think despite what the world says. If you don't know or don't think you are good at anything, that's okay. Yes, I know the "figuring it out" process is challenging, but I am *Matrix-level* confident you will keep peeling the onion to get to the core of what your true skill reality is. I recommend completing a career skills assessment (see the next chapter for a list of recommendations) and review the results with a friend or family member to help you with solving this uniquely personal mystery.

Once you have determined what your skills are, kick back and have a glass of wine or favorite exalted elixir (sorry, this strange word just means your drink of choice… I watched too many seasons of *Game of Thrones*[11]) to celebrate. After your celebration, you need to constantly improve your skills and amplify your value in the eyes of your co-workers, customers, and your boss. In my interview with Jesse, I was blown away at how she was able to leverage her resources, i.e. interns, and creativity to outmaneuver her colleagues to go on to win that

---

10   *The Matrix*, directed by Andy Wachowski and Larry Wachowski, (1999: Burbank, CA: Warner Bros. Pictures, 1999), DVD.

11   HBO Entertainment, *Game of Thrones*, 2012.

promotion. Jesse, if you are reading this, here is a virtual double high-five for that stroke of genius. Whether landing or interviewing for a job, you are always evaluated on whether or not you have the level of skills in order to perform in a way that meets the expectations of the customer, department, and company. Going to the DJ industry for a moment, yeah, there are some bad, good, and great DJs, but I bet the good and great ones constantly build their knowledge, techniques, and variety of skills all the time. Imagine ease-dropping on a conversation between two work friends at a happy hour with a live DJ playing: "Hey girl, what do you think of this music?" "I love it! DJ Rodney J is on-point. You know, the way he pulls it all together is so cool." This is the same sort of assessment conversation that happens about everyone in every profession between colleagues, managers, and customers on your performance based on your knowledge and skills. So, please be diligent on improving your knowledge and skills all the time.

KNOW WHAT BRINGS YOU PEACE

Knowing what brings you peace in this world is essential to your entire life. I am not going to spout quotes from the Dalai Lama or Pope Francis. Let's break it down in this way. If you are a college student, what is a peaceful feeling to you? Is it the thirty seconds after you catch your breath after a long run? Is it hearing the laughter of your friends as you smoke weed? Is it that early morning yawn when the sun is rising? Or, grabbing a Papa John's pizza with your family on a Friday night? If you are a millennial, what is your peace? Just grabbing a large cup of mocha from a boutique coffee shop after a hard day's work? Or is it being first in line at a popular spot for a happy hour with your co-workers? Or is it just taking a virtual meditation class after a long shower (oops, that is what I do)? Or is it just a standout comedy show (i.e. Ali Wong, Kevin Hart, Dave Chappell, or George Lopez get me laughing till my nose snots up…sorry for sharing too much.) If you are older than a millennial, I am sorry there is no peace for you—just kidding. All the things I threw out in the previous sentences for college students and millennials applies to all age categories. In my opinion, it is whatever helps you to relax deeply, to be harmonized, or just feel chilled out in a state of peace. I think it is a good idea to write down in a journal and keep at the top of your mind that you should try to feel peace several times a day, or ideally feel free as much as you can every day. Life is short, so live a life wrapped in as much peace as possible.

KNOW YOUR "ENERGY" ZONE

What I admired in my interview conversation with Connor at Jake's Coffee Shop was he seemed to have mastered knowing how to maximize shifting into his energy zone to achieve higher level of performance, client engagement, and pro-ductivity—which resulted in incredible success in his career. Being a morning person, I have noticed my brain is at its best during the wee hours of the morning light, I can work with greater accuracy when working on a project, reading dense material, or learning something new.

Also, I would say to my younger self that I have observed a plant-intensive diet, working with positive people, main-taining a growth mindset, and using as much creativity in the execution of most things at work and life is powerful in releasing the natural chemicals of the body to respond better, stronger, and adapt more dynamically to change in circumstances that happen in every job throughout our career.

BUILD YOUR CAREER TEAM

Ah, a career team, is the rocket fuel that powers every aspect your career. I have been fortunate to have a few wonderful people in my life that I can call right away for any situation at work or professional life in general. But I regret I didn't have these "call me anytime" career friends earlier in my career. Who should be on your career team? I recommend at least one mentor, former work colleagues, career coach, meditation teacher or religious leader, and a family mem ber (or good friend you have known for at least ten years). Each of the career team members play a critical role in your overall awareness of blind spots, emotional health, skill development, and ability to avoid the pitfalls that will slow your career progression.

A mentor or a few mentors can serve as advisers as you navigate the dark waters of your career, respond effectively to professional "storms," and make choices that will maximize your success and thrive on your job.

Former work colleagues are extremely valuable. The primary benefits of having a former colleague as a career team member are, they deeply know your personality, know how you have applied your skills in the workplace, and typically are in the same industry you are in. So, when you are needing a second opinion on a career change that you are thinking about making in your industry, they can perhaps share what they know to help you make a more informed decision in terms of the right job or company that would be great for you to consider.

A career coach is like Yoda (not baby Yoda) or a judo master. They act quickly to listen and absorb what needs to be learned about you, and effortlessly share knowledge aimed to develop your self-awareness, inspire clarity in how you think about your career situation, and empower you to make choices that align with you.

A meditation teacher or religious leader will allow you to better understand your spirit, and help to align your mind, body, and soul in a way to strengthen your sense of self. At times, one can be locked in an emotionally and spiritually abusive work environment and feel completely lost on what to do—especially when you are many levels beyond emotional numbness. I have been there, and often times, it seems easier to simply endure for years in some cases, but I encourage you to open up a dialogue with your meditation teacher or religious/spiritual leader to get some advice before enduring this pain. Also, here is where you can talk with other members of your career team before engaging in suffering that robs your sense of peace, success, and happiness in all areas of your work and personal life.

So, the family member or good friend serves in the role of a comforter and stress beater. When I have been overwhelmed with frustration or worry about a situation at work or considering to make a job change, I have found the deepest comfort during those painful times when I would talk with a good friend, parent, or one of my siblings.

CREATE THE IMPRESSION (FIRST IMPRESSIONS ARE EVERYTHING!)

I read somewhere that first impressions are created in two seconds. I believe this is probably true, and so, I think it would be wise to be intentional about the impression you want to create with every person you meet. People want to create a perception of who you are, and once established, rarely does it change from that initial impression.

KNOW HOW TO MOVE YOUR CROWD

It was always so cool to walk into a lounge, and see a large crowd being commanded by the thunderous voice of a DJ and bad ass, base heavy music, to dance on the small dance floor. When I attended wedding receptions, birthday parties, and a variety of celebrations, the DJ would know how to encourage people to dance, relax, and enjoy the music. Obviously, we can't command anyone to do anything at work, but we can influence others to take action, lead, and certainly influence the decision-making process. What I wish I could tell my younger self is you need to learn how to influence co-workers, customers, and your boss in a way that will significantly magnify the belief you are the MVP of the department. You want to make them believe if there was an MVP award you should be the one to receive it. On the other hand, I totally understand if such a distinction is not what you want, tin that case, define for yourself how you would like to influence others, and work on achieving that level of influencing on a regular basis.

Imagine you are working a long day in hopes of getting something accomplished, yet no matter how hard you are working, time is moving faster than you can work. Seven, nine, eleven, and fourteen hours go by, and finally at the seventeenth hour, you finally finish what needs to be done for that project. Or, if a co-worker quits the job, and all of their work is "temporarily" assigned to you. You feel like you have been punched in the face or gut every day you are enduring this ridiculous work overload for seemingly an indefinite time. If this level of overwork and overstress is more like a fifteen round boxing match that pushes you to your limit on a regular basis, talk with your career team to get their opinion and take the necessary action.

JUMP INTO THE VOLCANO (NOT LITERALLY)

In the early 1990s, I watched a fantastic soul-stirring romantic movie, *Joe versus the Volcano*, starring Tom Hanks and Meg Ryan.[12] If you haven't seen the movie, and now you are intrigued enough to want to watch it, then skip this little section in the chapter. Spoiler alert! Basically, Joe (Tom) is mistakenly told he has six months to live. Because of this diagnosis, Joe immediately becomes extremely present and urgent about what is most important to him in the seemingly last days of his life. He quits his job, then asks Meg out on a date. Joe becomes not only bold, but fearless and purpose-driven about what he wants to experience in his "short" life. Eventually he agrees to jump in a volcano on a tiny island in the south pacific in exchange for a life of riches and luxury. The wealthy man offering this deal will receive some rare minerals from the island's natives if Joe jumps. There

---

12   *Joe Versus the Volcano*, directed by John Patrick Shanley (1990: Burbank, CA: Warner Bros. Pictures, 2007), DVD.

are other elements of this movie's story worth shining a light on it, but the transformation of Joe is critical to the idea we need to live with greater urgency in every aspect of our life, because the future isn't promised to anyone. Imagine living a life where you attacked your goals and dreams with a "life or death" sense of urgency that wakes you up early in the morning and doesn't easily go away at night; but rather it is a force of nature that compels you to work smarter, harder, and faster each day, because every day could be your last. In case you are wondering, Joe does jump into the volcano, survives, and thrives as a new person.

LIFT UP OTHERS IN YOUR COMMUNITY

While growing up, I remember a super funny and patient young man who spent a few hours at the Junior Achievement—a non-profit committed to teaching business skills through making and selling a product. I learned a lot about what it meant to work on a team, create something of value, and learned how to sell for the first time in my life. Many of the kids in my neighborhood went to the Boys and Girls Club or Junior Achievement. We found peace, play, and self-discovery. I feel like we were growing into something special like each pear on my pear tree in my backyard. I felt like we were growing, learning, and gaining confidence because of our self-expression. As I think about who I am today, I think it was great people who were committed to lifting up someone like me as a young teenager is the reason I am who I am today. I think investing your time by teaching, helping, or sharing your sense of humor with kids, the elderly, or people with physical disabilities will serve to actually strengthen your heart and mind in ways that are difficult to express.

FREE YOUR "INNER DJ"

Yes, yes, and yes… please grow your "inner DJ," this is the extremely creative, resourceful, dynamically aware, and emotionally passionate nature fights from within to challenge you to freestyle with creativity, draw inspiration from others, and constantly pushes you to be more dynamic in pursuing what is important to you. If you woke up one morning in a hotel room in San Paulo, Brazil, or any non-English speaking foreign country, it would be your "inner DJ" that would kick in to help you get out of this crazy situation without losing your mind in the process. I think when we embrace living life with boldness, conviction, and big impact we are nurturing the growth of a "inner DJ" mindset that mixes, spins, frequency volumes, and beat matches your approach to work, life, and how you impact others.

As light is refracted through a prism to create a wide spectrum of colors, I believe if you develop the "inner DJ" in your mind and soul in order to help you realize the spectrum of thinking at your disposal, to empower your underlying decision-making, and learn how you manage your career, the possibilities for your career's trajectory are boundless. This "inner DJ" is the common element I have found in so many of the people I have interviewed. I think it exists in all of us, but we need to be inspired, awakened, and driven to the reality of tapping into it.

CHAPTER 18

ADDITIONAL RESOURCES FOR THE READER

THOUGHT-INSPIRING MOVIES

Coogler, Ryan, dir. *Creed.*

Crowe, Cameron, dir. *Jerry Maguire.*

Levy, Shawn, dir. *The Internship.*

Luketic, Robert, dir. *Legally Blonde.*

Melfi, Theodore, dir. *Hidden Figures.*

Muccino, Gabriele, dir. *The Pursuit of Happyness.*

Ramis, Harold, dir. *Groundhog Day.*

Reitman, Jason, dir. *Up in the Air.*

Van Sant, Gus, dir. *Good Will Hunting.*

BOOKS

Bolles, Richard. *What Color is Your Parachute?* Berkley: Ten Speed Press, 2015.

Bonetti, Benjamin. *How to Stress Less: Simple Ways to Stop Worrying and Take Control of Your Future.* Chichester, UK: John Wiley and Sons Ltd., 2014.

Burnett, Bill and Dave Evans. *Designing Your Work Life: How to Thrive and Change and Find Happiness at Work.* New York: Alfred A. Knoph, 2020.

Carnegie, Dale. *How to Win Friends and Influence People.* New York: Simon & Schuster, 2009.

Coelho, Paulo. *The Alchemist.* San Francisco: HarperSanFrancisco, 1998.

Dweck, Carol S. *Mindset: The New Psychology of Success.* Updated ed. New York: Penguin Random House LLC, 2016.

Gardner, Chris and Mim Eichler Rivas. *Start Where You Are: Life Lessons in Getting from Where You are to Where You Want to Be.* New York: Harper Collins, 2009.

Tieger, Paul, Barbara Barron, and Kelly Tieger. *Do What You Are.* 5th ed. New York: Little, Brown and Company, 2014

Sincero, Jen. *You Are a Badass.* Series. New York: Penguin Random House LLC, 2013, 2018.

WEBSITES

www.linkedin.com

https://www.themuse.com/

https://www.parachutebook.com/

https://rpilib.org/best-free-online-libraries/

https://www.indeed.com/

https://www.glassdoor.com/

https://angel.co/

https://www.flexjobs.com

PODCASTS

Blake, Jenny. *Pivot*. Podcast, MP3 audio.

Guillebeau, Chris. *Side Hustle School*. Podcast, MP3 audio.

Howes, Lewis. *The School of Greatness*. Podcast, MP3 audio.

McClinton, Nathan. *The Gifted Connection*. Podcast, MP3 audio.

McGinn, Dan and Alison Beard. *Dear HBR*. Podcast, MP3 audio.

Taha, Hala. *Young and Profiting*. Podcast, MP3 audio.

Toure Show. *Toure Show*. Podcast, MP3 audio.

AMAZING TED TALKS

Cuddy, Amy. "Your Body Language May Shape Who You Are." TED talk. June 2012.

Harris, Carol. "How to Find the Person Who Can Help You Get Ahead at Work." TED Talk. November 2018.

Lopez, Shane. "The Secrets of People Who Love their Jobs." TEDx talk. June 2015.

Shen, Jason. "When Looking for a Job, Highlight Your Ability Not Your Experience." TED talk. November 2017.

Sinek, Simon. "How Great Leaders Inspire Action." TEDx talk. September 2009.

Tasner, Paul. "How I Became an Entrepreneur at 66." TED talk. June 2017.

Rhimes, Shonda. "My Year of Saying Yes to Everything." TED talk. February 2016.

APPENDIX

———

PREFACE

Boseman, Chadwick. "Commencement Speech: What You Fight For." May 12, 2018, Howard University. https://www.englishspeecheschannel.com/english-speeches/chadwick-boseman-speech/.

CHAPTER ONE

Glassdoor Team. "50 HR and Recruiting Stats that Make You Think." *Glassdoor.* January 20, 2015. https://www.glassdoor.com/employers/blog/50-hr-recruiting-stats-make-think/

CHAPTER TWO

Crabtree, Steve. "Worldwide, 13% of Employees Are Engaged at Work." *Gallup News.* October 8, 2013. https://news.gallup.com/poll/165269/worldwide-employees-engaged-work.aspx.

Pink, Daniel. *Drive: The Surprising Truth About What Motivates Us*. New York: Riverhead Books, 2009.

The Conference Board. "Job Satisfaction: 2014 Edition." 2014. https://www.conference-board.org/research/job-satisfaction/job-satisfaction-2014.

Your Coach. "Health Coaching Industry Report: Aiding at the Frontlines of Health." 2020. https://yourcoach.health/healthcoachingreport/health-coaching-report-yourcoach.pdf.

CHAPTER TEN

BBC. *The Man with No Name*. BBC, 1977.

Eastwood, Clint, dir. *Pale Rider*. Malpaso Creek, CA: The Malpaso Company, 1985.

Leone, Sergio, dir. *For a Few Dollars More*. Produzioni Europee Associati, 1965.

CHAPTER ELEVEN

Wachowski, Lana, dir. *The Matrix*. Burbank, CA: Warner Brothers, 1999.

CHAPTER THIRTEEN

Tyler, Kathryn. "How to Find the Right HR Mentor." *SHRM*. April 16, 2018. https://www.shrm.org/hr-today/news/hr-magazine/0518/pages/how-to-find-the-right-hr-mentor.aspx.

CHAPTER SEVENTEEN

HBO Entertainment. *Game of Thrones: The Complete First Season*. New York: HBO Entertainment, 2012.

Shanley, John Patrick, dir. *Joe Versus the Volcano*. Burbank, CA: Warner Brothers Entertainment, 1990.

Wachowski, Lana, dir. *The Matrix*. Burbank, CA: Warner Brothers, 1999.